EXTREME SPORTS

BIG AIR
SNOWBOARDING

BY THOMAS K. ADAMSON

EPIC

BELLWETHER MEDIA • MINNEAPOLIS, MN

EPIC

EPIC BOOKS are no ordinary books. They burst with intense action, high-speed heroics, and shadows of the unknown. Are you ready for an Epic adventure?

This edition first published in 2016 by Bellwether Media, Inc.

No part of this publication may be reproduced in whole or in part without written permission of the publisher. For information regarding permission, write to Bellwether Media, Inc., Attention: Permissions Department, 5357 Penn Avenue South, Minneapolis, MN 55419.

Library of Congress Cataloging-in-Publication Data

Adamson, Thomas K., 1970-
  Big Air Snowboarding / by Thomas K. Adamson.
     pages cm. – (Epic: Extreme Sports)
  Includes bibliographical references and index.
  Summary: "Engaging images accompany information about big air snowboarding. The combination of high-interest subject matter and light text is intended for students in grades 2 through 7"– Provided by publisher.
  Audience: Grades: 2 through 7.
  ISBN 978-1-62617-351-4 (hardcover : alk. paper)
  1. Snowboarding–Juvenile literature. 2. Extreme sports–Juvenile literature. 3. ESPN X-Games–Juvenile literature. I. Title.
  GV857.S57A37 2016
  796.939–dc23
                              2015028735

Printed in the United States of America, North Mankato, MN.

TABLE OF CONTENTS

WARNING

The tricks shown in this book are
performed by professionals. Always
wear a helmet and other safety gear
when you are on a snowboard.

SPINNING FOR GOLD

Six snowboarders take turns flying off a huge ramp. This is the Snowboard Big Air event at the Winter X Games. Mark McMorris nails a Frontside Triple Cork 1440. The crowd cheers his daring trick.

McMorris needs another gnarly trick to help him win. He lands a Backside Triple Cork 1620. The judges give him the best score of the night. He wins X Games gold!

HAD TO GO FOR IT!
McMorris had never landed the Backside Triple Cork 1620 before the 2015 Winter X Games.

BIG AIR SNOWBOARDING

Big air snowboarding is all about huge tricks. Riders speed down a steep hill. They reach up to 50 miles (80 kilometers) per hour. Then they jump off the ramp at the end.

9

Big air snowboarding ramps can be built in cities. Sometimes they are even built indoors.

Riders can fly 100 feet (30 meters) above the ground. This distance allows a lot of air time for a creative trick.

BIG AIR SNOWBOARDING TERMS

Backside Triple Cork 1620—a trick in which the rider does three flips while spinning backward four and one-half times in the air

Frontside Triple Cork 1440—a trick in which the rider does three flips while spinning forward four times in the air

grab—a trick in which the rider holds the board with one hand while doing the trick

jam format—a snowboarding contest in which riders take many turns doing tricks within a set amount of time

Switch Quadruple Underflip 1620—a trick in which the rider flips backward four times and lands with the back foot forward

BIG AIR BEGINNINGS

Freestyle riders created big air snowboarding in the 1990s. They wanted an event for trying difficult new tricks. From 1997 to 2001, the Winter X Games featured Snowboard Big Air. Then fans had to wait until 2008 for its return.

1997 Summer X Games

SUMMER SNOWBOARDING

In the late 1990s, Snowboard Big Air was also held at the Summer X Games. Man-made snow covered the ramp.

2013 Snowboard World Cup

VW Das Auto.

Red Bull MOBILE

PROVINCIE ANTWERPEN

2012 Snowboard
World Cup

Today, big air competitions are more
popular than ever. Since the early 2000s,
the Snowboard World Cup has included
big air. The event has also been added to
the 2018 Winter Olympics.

BIG AIR GEAR

Helmets and goggles are required in big air snowboarding. Goggles protect eyes from snow and sun. Big air boards are more flexible and shorter than other snowboards.

WAX FOR SPEED
Smooth wax covers the bottom of snowboards. This helps them glide over snow.

THE COMPETITION

Most big air snowboarding events have a jam format. Riders perform one trick after another. Judges award points for each trick. Riders can score up to 50 points per trick.

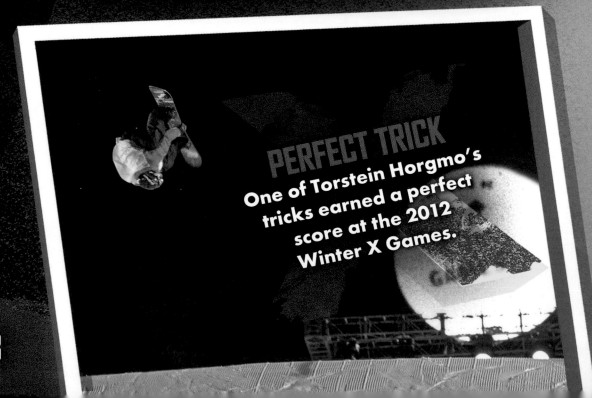

PERFECT TRICK

One of Torstein Horgmo's tricks earned a perfect score at the 2012 Winter X Games.

EVENT SCORING

Big air snowboarding tricks are judged on their height and difficulty. Grabs and spins make tricks more difficult. Riders who show control during their tricks also score higher.

Competitions begin with qualifying rounds. Each rider's two best scores are added. The top scoring riders move on to the finals. The rider in the finals with the highest combined score wins!

INNOVATOR OF THE SPORT

name: **Maxence Parrot**
birthdate: **June 6, 1994**
hometown: **Bromont, Quebec, Canada**
innovations: **Landed the first Switch Quadruple Underflip 1620 and won 4 X Games snowboarding medals**

GLOSSARY

competitions—events that snowboarders try to win

creative—having new ideas or doing something a different way

flexible—able to bend

gnarly—cool and awesome; gnarly often describes a difficult trick.

qualifying rounds—early parts of a competition; riders with the highest scores move through the qualifying rounds.

steep—almost straight up and down

trick—a specific move in a Snowboard Big Air event

TO LEARN MORE

AT THE LIBRARY

Benjamin, Daniel. *Extreme Snowboarding*. New York, N.Y.: Marshall Cavendish Benchmark, 2012.

Hile, Lori. *The Science of Snowboarding*. North Mankato, Minn.: Capstone Press, 2014.

Mason, Paul. *Snowboarding*. Chicago, Ill.: Raintree, 2014.

ON THE WEB

Learning more about big air snowboarding is as easy as 1, 2, 3.

1. Go to www.factsurfer.com.

2. Enter "big air snowboarding" into the search box.

3. Click the "Surf" button and you will see a list of related web sites.

With factsurfer.com, finding more information is just a click away.

INDEX

The images in this book are reproduced through the courtesy of: Action Plus Sports Images/ Alamy, front cover; Agence Zoom/ Stringer/ Getty Images, pp. 5, 6-7, 20; Mathieu Belanger/ Reuters/ Newscom, p. 8; Jeff Smith/ Perspectives, p. 9; Associated Press, p. 10, 15, 21 (bottom); Nurlan Kalchinov, p. 11; Robert Beck/ Getty Images (Sports Illustrated collection), p. 13; Panoramic/ Zuma Press/ Newscom, p. 14; Mark Esper/ Polaris/ Newscom, p. 16; Lisi Niesner/ Stringer/ Getty Images, p. 17 (left); Yarygin, p. 17 (right); Rustin Gudim/ Zuma Press/ Newscom, p. 18; Dominic Steinmann/ Getty Images, p. 19; Imago/ Zuma Press, p. 21 (top).